**MARK L. MADRID**

# ENERGY

## 21 Uncomplicated & Easy Tips
### to Start Your Day Energized by 9 AM

Book Series on Self-Fueling Excellence

# ENERGY

© Copyright 2024, Mark L. Madrid
All rights reserved.

All rights reserved. No portion of this book may be reproduced by mechanical, photographic or electronic process, nor may it be stored in a retrieval system, transmitted in any form or otherwise be copied for public use or private use without written permission of the copyright owner.

**Published by**
Fig Factor Media, LLC | www.figfactormedia.com

Cover Design & Layout by Juan Pablo Ruiz

*Printed in the United States of America*

**ISBN: 978-1-959989-92-9**
**Library of Congress Control Number: 2024913790**

# DEDICATION

*This book is wholeheartedly dedicated to my mother, Maria Madrid. A woman of extraordinary tenacity, she has selflessly devoted her life to her children. As she bravely navigates through a series of major challenges, I pray specifically that she claims and fuels her epic tenacity and grit. These are the principles that I am privileged to have inherited from her and my father, and they serve as pillars of this book series. My deepest hope is that she fully recognizes and embraces these qualities within herself, just as they have profoundly shaped my life and work. This book is not just a testament to these principles but also a tribute to her life, as I was formed from her.*

# ACKNOWLEDGMENTS

First, my heartfelt thanks go to you, the reader. Your commitment to self-improvement and excellence is the driving force behind this book series. I sincerely appreciate your time, investment, and pursuit of Self-Fueled Excellence!

This book series is a perpetual testament to my enduring empathy, strong connection to the ground, and signature energy, discipline, and grit. I hope that through these pages, you draw inspiration and—most importantly—act to break through.

I express my profound gratitude to my partner, Dan, for his unwavering love and steadfast support. I also honor the memory of my father, Marcos Madrid, Jr., whose inspiring legacy lives on through my actions.

My sisters, Mary and Diana and my niece Neely have been my pillars of love and strength. I devote a special shout-out to Champ, whose unconditional love does not go unnoticed. And, my ride-or-die tribeAG, I couldn't do this without you.

I pay tribute to Oprah Winfrey, whose authentic and inspiring journey has had an unspeakable impact on me, lifting me from dark places into victory. Oprah, I don't know you, but I feel like you know me. THANK YOU.

I hope you, the reader, and those around you will reap a bountiful harvest from these core principles. When combined, these principles can lead to unimaginable breakthroughs. This accessible belief system is the inspiration behind my recent venture, Breakthrough Mavens, LLC, offering fractional C-Suite services, and the overall launch of the Mark L. Madrid brand.

Finally, I acknowledge my alma maters, the University of Texas at Austin and the University of Notre Dame, as well as Texas State University. The education and experiences I gained there have been instrumental in unleashing excellence. Remember, no one can take your education from you. Always keep learning.

Onward to your Self-Fueling Excellence!

# INTRODUCTION

Welcome to the first book of the Self-Fueling Excellence Series, *ENERGY: Increasing Your Energy with 21 Uncomplicated, Meaningful, and Simple Solutions by 9 A.M.* This book is more than just a guide; it's a journey toward becoming the best version of yourself, fueled by energy, discipline, and grit.

My declaration of accomplishments by 9 a.m. is a lasting tribute to a former U.S. Army campaign that proudly stated, 'We do more by 9 a.m. than most people do all day.' This homage not only reflects my respect for the discipline and efficiency of our armed forces but also my personal honor of being named an honorary colonel by the U.S. Army. It serves as a daily reminder of the commitment, energy, and discipline that define both the military and my approach to life.

This book is not only about sharing tips but also about sharing my life philosophy as an overcomer. This proven philosophy is built on three primary pillars: energy, discipline, and grit. They are not just words but principles that have guided me through my journey and shaped me into the human I am today.

This book is the first in a series of three, with the next two focusing on grit and discipline, respectively.

But before we delve into those, we start with energy. Energy is the driving force that propels us forward. It's the spark that ignites our passion, fuels our discipline, and gives us the grit to overcome challenges.

Each point made is a step towards harnessing your energy and channeling it towards your success. They are uncomplicated, meaningful, and simple solutions anyone can incorporate into their daily routine. Whether you're at the peak of your life or going through a challenging time, these points are hopefully relatable and adaptable to your unique journey.

This book is dedicated to my mother, Maria Madrid, a woman of incredible strength and resilience who is currently fighting through a series of challenges. We hope she takes advantage of her courage, tenacity, and grit, principles that I have inherited and that have shaped my book series.

Above all, this book is about hope. It's about believing in your potential, embracing your journey, and knowing that no matter what, #SuccessIsPossible. It's about understanding that a whole lot of little goes a long way, and that every step you take, no matter how small, brings you closer to your purpose and fulfillment.

So, as you turn these pages, remember: You can take control of your own life. You have the power to shape your day, your life, your story. Claim your energy, embrace the journey, and go forth and win the day!

Let's begin this journey together.

**Replace snooze with activation and this first thought, "This awakening moment marks the first day of the rest of my life, and I have control of how I BEGIN this day before the world—with its opportunities and challenges—tries to take over."**

Ignite your day, don't snooze it away! The moment you wake up is truly a moment of your power, an instant representing a fresh start. Before other forces and/or people, you have this instant and awesome opportunity to determine how you paint this partially blank canvas.

Instead of delaying the start of your day with the snooze button, seize this moment as an opportunity for self-activation. Treat this moment as the first day of the rest of your life, and you have control of how you BEGIN this day before the world—with its opportunities and challenges—tries to take over. This simple shift can set a powerful tone for the rest of your day, putting you in the driver's seat.

Simply step into your power and potential rather than permitting outside forces to dictate your mood and actions.

Here is an inspiring quote that encourages us to view each new day as an opportunity to gather our strength and courage, just like the sun does as it rises.

> *"The sun himself is weak when he first rises and gathers strength and courage as the day gets on."* **—Charles Dickens**

**Treat YOU with a #PositiveAffirmation. For me, it is the Serenity Prayer, "God grant me the serenity to accept the things I cannot change; courage to change the things I can; and wisdom to know the difference."**

Treating yourself with a #PositiveAffirmation is a powerful way to start your day. You will nourish your morning mind by providing it with a boost of self-driven optimism. For me, the Serenity Prayer serves as that affirmation. It's a beautiful prayer that encapsulates a profound truth about life and our place in it.

"God grant me the serenity to accept the things I cannot change; courage to change the things I can; and wisdom to know the difference." This prayer is a reminder that not everything is within our control. There are things we must learn to accept. While there are elements in life that remain beyond our control, there are indeed aspects that we hold the power to transform. The wisdom lies in knowing the difference. This most liberating discernment can deliver that treasured peace of mind.

#TakeControlOfYourOwnLife, and first a.m. is an undeniable and consistent moment for you to self-direct meaningful momentum in your own words.

Consider this quote and remember to not only recite your positive affirmations but to live them out each day.

> *"Be the change that you wish to see in the world."*
> —Mahatma Gandhi

**No Screens: They will soon dominate your day, so dominate them when you can, which is upon awakening. Make this moment about YOU. #YouAreInControlOfFirstAM**

Please imagine a moment, one in which you choose to be free of the digital barrage, which can potentially trigger negativity, conflict, anxiety, or spiraling thoughts. Those negative thoughts can outrun those precious positive ones. One of the greatest permissions is one you grant to yourself. In this case, try at least thirty minutes free from potential external mind debris. How about this? Thirty minutes accounts for approximately only 2 percent of your day. Choose you over screens during this sacred early a.m. time.

#YouAreInControlOfFirstAM is not just a hashtag; it's a mantra, a reminder that you have the power to shape your day, starting with the very first hour. In no time—integrating simple discipline tips—you will embark on a lifestyle pivot, built by micro-moments of undistracted mind-body-spirit space that can renaissance your life. I should know because this simple tactic has produced daily clarity that keeps my priorities front and center and distractions in the parking lot!

Life is meant to be lived with intention and to the fullest.

> *"Successful people maintain a positive focus in life no matter what is going on around them."* —**Jack Canfield**

**Embrace the Light: This simple #Habit of receiving the sunshine or turning on your lights will help regulate your internal clock. #YouAreInControlOfYourCadence**

Embracing the light is about more than just turning on a lamp or opening a curtain. It's about aligning yourself with your body's natural rhythms and the day. Our bodies have an internal clock, known as the circadian rhythm, which is heavily influenced by light. When light enters our eyes, it sends a signal to our brain to stop producing melatonin, a hormone that helps us sleep. This helps regulate our sleep-wake cycle and aligns us with the natural rhythms of the day.

This one-to-grown-on simple #Habit can profoundly affect your energy levels, mood, and overall health.

#IAMInControlOfMyCadence is a powerful affirmation. Embrace the light, literally turn on physiological benefits, and invigorate your atmosphere, including the one within. Let the light in (and "in").

Remember to embrace the light not only physically but also metaphorically by focusing on the positive and beautiful aspects of life.

> *"Durkness cannot drive out darkness, only light can do that.*
> *Hate cannot drive out hate: only love can do that."*
> **—Dr. Martin Luther King**

**Splash Water on Your Face: It works! Invigorate tired eyes and dehydrated skin and symbolically water (nourish) your spirit.**

This simple act works! For me, splashing cool water on my face is not just a physical act, but it is a symbolic one, as well. This daily #Habit invigorates my eyes and rehydrates my skin. At the beginning and end of the day, water is symbolic of life, renewal, and nourishment. Also, according to healthline.com, a quick facial cleanse in the a.m. is recommended due to the notable bacteria on pillowcases.

#ItWorks is a testament to the effectiveness of this simple act. It's a reminder that sometimes the simplest acts can have profound effects.

This daily practice can inspire you to not only splash cool water on your face but also to embrace the qualities of water, fluidity, softness, and strength in your life.

> "Water is fluid, soft, and yielding. But water will wear away rock, which is rigid and cannot yield. As a rule, whatever is fluid, soft, and yielding will overcome whatever is rigid and hard. This is another paradox: what is soft is strong."
> —Lao Tzu, Chinese philosopher and writer

**More H2O—Drink Two Glasses of Water: No reason not to hydrate first thing! The bonus: You will boost your metabolism!**

I'll be honest and vulnerable. I've persevered through cycles of weight gain and loss in different eras of my life. When hitting the mark with both nutrition and fitness, water intake has been the common denominator of success every time! Hydration is key to our health and well-being, yet we often overlook it. Try kick-starting your day with two noteworthy glasses of water first thing in the morning.

Why not hydrate first thing? This habit has numerous benefits, including boosting your metabolism, replenishing your body after sleep, and aiding your digestion.

If your goal is to drink eight glasses of water daily, you will be 25 percent to the goal by 9 a.m. I ascribe to the #FrontLoadingPrinciple, which involves doing things sooner rather than later and mitigating delay and/or procrastination. This simple and uncomplicated principle has saved me countless times, professionally and personally.

In this case, it is all for health, and investing in your health should be one of your highest priorities, both for you and the loved ones around you.

> *"Water is the driving force of all nature."* —**Leonardo da Vinci**

**Play Your Favorite Uplifting Song: #PositveThoughts over negative thoughts.**

Music has the power to ignite our souls. Starting your day with one of your favorite uplifting songs can set a positive tone for the rest of the day.

For me, one of those songs is "Greatest Love of All," the version by Whitney Houston.

This song has emerged for me as a powerful anthem for loving and believing in yourself. Simply playing this song reminds me (every time) of my journey of sheer grit, resilience, determination, and victory.

Therefore, playing this song first thing in the morning (which I often do) helps my mind, body (more later), and spirit. It uplifts me, paints that partially blank morning canvas with an uplifting representation of self, and definitely results in a spring in my steps!

I invite you to fuel your imagination and spirit with uplifting music every morning before you leave the house.

*"Music gives a soul to the universe, wings to the mind, flight to the imagination, and life to everything."* —**Plato**

**Start Your Day with a Win: Make Your Bed! Every accomplishment, no matter how big or small, is a win. Within minutes of awakening, make your bed and #CollectTheWin.**

One of the simplest yet most powerful habits you can adopt is making your bed first thing in the morning. This small act, accomplished within minutes of waking up, sets the tone for the day. It's a testament to your ability to take control of your environment and complete a task, no matter how small. The added bonus: this tip integrates seamlessly with the others in this book.

Every accomplishment, big or small, is a victory nonetheless! By making your bed, you're starting your day with a win and a positive affirmation that you took initiative. Simple acts like this one fuel a #WinningMindset.

This concept is not new. As an honors graduate from the University of Texas at Austin, I find this next quote particularly resonant. Make your bed every morning, and start your day feeling like a winner!

> *"If you want to change the world, start off by making your bed."*
> **—Admiral William H. McRaven, former chancellor of the University of Texas System and a decorated U.S. Navy officer**

**Dance or Exercise: Do it first thing; in just a few minutes, it can revolutionize your life and become a #BestYouHabit as you #UnleashYourEndorphins and mark #AnotherEarlyMorningAccomplishment. For me, it is T25 with Shaun T.**

Starting your day with any type of movement, whether walking briskly, dancing, and/or exercising, sends a powerful message to yourself that you are investing in your energy and metabolism. Over the long haul, just a few minutes every day can make a significant difference.

By implementing this simple, no-cost tip, you will not only move your body but also release endorphins, the body's natural mood lifters.

Transform a fleeting moment into an active and fun one! #UnleashYourEndorphins in the first a.m. and tap into your body's natural ability to make you feel good.

For me, T25 with Shaun T is my go-to every morning. This high-intensity, quick workout is my reliable and consistent daily kickstarter, no matter the circumstance, rain or shine! It has proven effective during my most exhilarating times and the most traumatic times, too.

Trust me. This is a no-cost/low cost and simple anti-aging solution.

> *"Take care of your body. It's the only place you have to live."*
> —Jim Rohn, entrepreneur and author

**Eat: Why put off nourishing your body and brain? Kickstart with a healthy option, because it might be harder or more complicated to access later.**

#FrontLoadYourDay (back to the #FrontLoadingPrinciple) with fueling your body and mind with an uncomplicated and healthy breakfast. After years of not adhering to this simple principle, I transformed my life by simply integrating an easy, portable, pre-planned, low-cost, nutritious breakfast option after a night's sleep. This may not work for all. For me, I have relied on this #SelfFuel to kickstart my body and nourish my brain.

Often, starting the day with a nutritious option has motivated me to continue healthy eating throughout the day. Can you relate to the following voice (#Truth), which has often whispered in my ear, "Well, Mark, you enjoyed those three donuts . . . you might as well make this a cheat day!" I can't count how many times I have fallen victim to this self-voice of #BadInspiration. Fortunately, because of my #Discipline (coming soon!), the self-voice of #GoodInspiration has conquered the self-voice of #BadInspiration more often than not, which has made a huge difference.

An example of one of my healthy breakfast options is an egg white breakfast taco made with Ole Mexican Foods Xtreme Wellness! High Fiber CARB LEAN tortilla with crushed red pepper flakes and a sprinkle of fat-free natural mozzarella shredded cheese.

What are three possible options for you?

> *"Let food be thy medicine and medicine be thy food."* —**Hippocrates**

**What is that one small thing that is IMPORTANT TO YOU that you must do TODAY to be successful? When you achieve this small thing, you can mark this day as a success! #SuccessIsPossible when we break it down into manageable parts.**

This principle has been a personal game-changer! It has influenced exponential trajectory in both my professional and personal lives. Indeed, this question is a most powerful one. What TRULY matters to you? What is that #OneThing—when accomplished today—that would make you feel accomplished because you advanced a #SelfPriority today?

What is magical—but not coincidental—about this simple tip is that this #OneThing can be small! Breaking News: Success is not always about monumental and grandiose achievements but often about small, meaningful actions.

#OneToGrowOn: For me, when breaking down a huge #MovingMountain, #BigRockGoal into manageable parts has often resulted in resonating and enduring success. Life's greatest achievements don't come through shortcuts. The victory is sweeter when it is earned.

When writing this particular passage, I decided that #OneThing for me today was to complete one business proposal that is in #AlmostFinished mode.

What is that #OneThing for you?

What is reassuring about this tip, as with all the others in this book: #ItIsDoable

Implementing this simple tip will ensure you are not underestimating your simple wins, which—when aggregated—lead to the big win.

> *"Success is the sum of small efforts, repeated day in and day out."*
> **—Robert Collier, author**

**Write, text, or call someone that you love before you walk out the door.**

This is a beautiful practice, plain and simple. It's about making time for the people who matter most to you, even amid a challenging and busy morning. When you start the day with love, you can't go wrong.

What is more important than connecting with those whom matter the most to you? Who are the five or ten people that mean the most to you?

The bottom line is that this one pure and simple practice has ensured that the most important people in my life know with certainty that they are important and loved. When my family was ravished with COVID-19, and we lost our dad (and almost mom), the harsh reality hit me like a ton of bricks. I was not calling mom and dad enough.

Now, I call my mom every single day without fail, and express my deep love.

Start your day with love, as this simple act of kindness can make a big and #GreatDifference in someone's day. I've never met anyone who didn't appreciate feeling valued.

Imagine expressing love every morning. Truly, it is a win-win, a win for you and a win for the one you love.

> *"Spread love everywhere you go. Let no one ever come to you without leaving happier."* —**Mother Teresa**

**What is one thing that you are grateful for? Record it on your phone notes, audio notes, and/or gratitude journal.**

This powerful question can shift your focus from what's going wrong to what's going right, even if what's going right is just one thing. Gratitude has been linked to scores of benefits for #MindBodySpirit.

Caution: In my experience, negative thoughts have run faster than positive ones in big moments.

The solution: Over time, with #SelfDiscipline, I have trained myself to record what I'm grateful for daily. I don't overcomplicate this. Today, it could be a text to myself (yes, you can do that). Tomorrow, it could be on my whiteboard in my bathroom. The next day, it could be a voice note. As well, I have a simple gratitude journal. One of my meaningful #Breakthroughs has been reflecting on gratitude journal entries from the past. There is power and learning in #ReReveals.

This practice is about more than just feeling good. It's about training your mind to focus on the positive and appreciate the good in your life. It's a small act with big benefits, not only for you but also for those around you.

> *"Gratitude can transform any situation. It alters your vibration, moving you from negative energy to positive."* —**Oprah Winfrey**

**Write, text, or call someone that you should update. It's not only what you know and who you know, but what they know about you right now. Don't assume they know.**

Take control of your own narrative, both professionally and personally. At times, these narratives are interwoven, which further underscores the importance of this straightforward tip. Don't wait for others to share the most important things about you!

You are the best author of your own story: for your significant other, for your family, for your professional peers, and for your friends. Don't wait for others to learn about your key achievements or updates. Or, in some cases, when you need encouragement the most, reach out to that role model/mentor/confidant and present your challenges before they hear a distorted version from social media or someone else.

It's best coming from you authentically and in real-time.

Trust me; this principle has helped me win the constant battle of insecurity (#Truth #StrengthInVulnerability). Reveal yourself to those you trust the most.

So, as we wrap up this section, let's echo this powerful mantra once more: "It's not only what you know, but who you know and what they know about you right now!" Carry this wisdom with you, apply it in your daily life, and witness the transformative power it holds—not only for you, but those who champion you.

**Identify #OneThing that is challenging you and record it.**

This is a powerful practice that encourages self-awareness and #Truth. We all face challenges, but we often don't take the time to clearly identify and record those challenges. By identifying one thing challenging you, you're taking the first step towards addressing it. For me, that has been a huge weight lifted off my shoulders. In vulnerability, there is strength.

Recording this challenge on your phone notes, audio notes, or in a worry journal is a great way to acknowledge it and track your progress over time. It's a tangible reminder of what you're working on and can serve as a source of #SelfMotivation to overcome this challenge and others. In my life, this small act of #SelfTraining over time with #Discipline has empowered me to think of any challenge, big or small, as inevitably conquerable. Trust me; it is now firmly implanted in my being. #MustardSeed

> "Challenges are what make life interesting, and overcoming them is what makes life meaningful."
> —Joshua J. Marine, magician, author, and lecturer

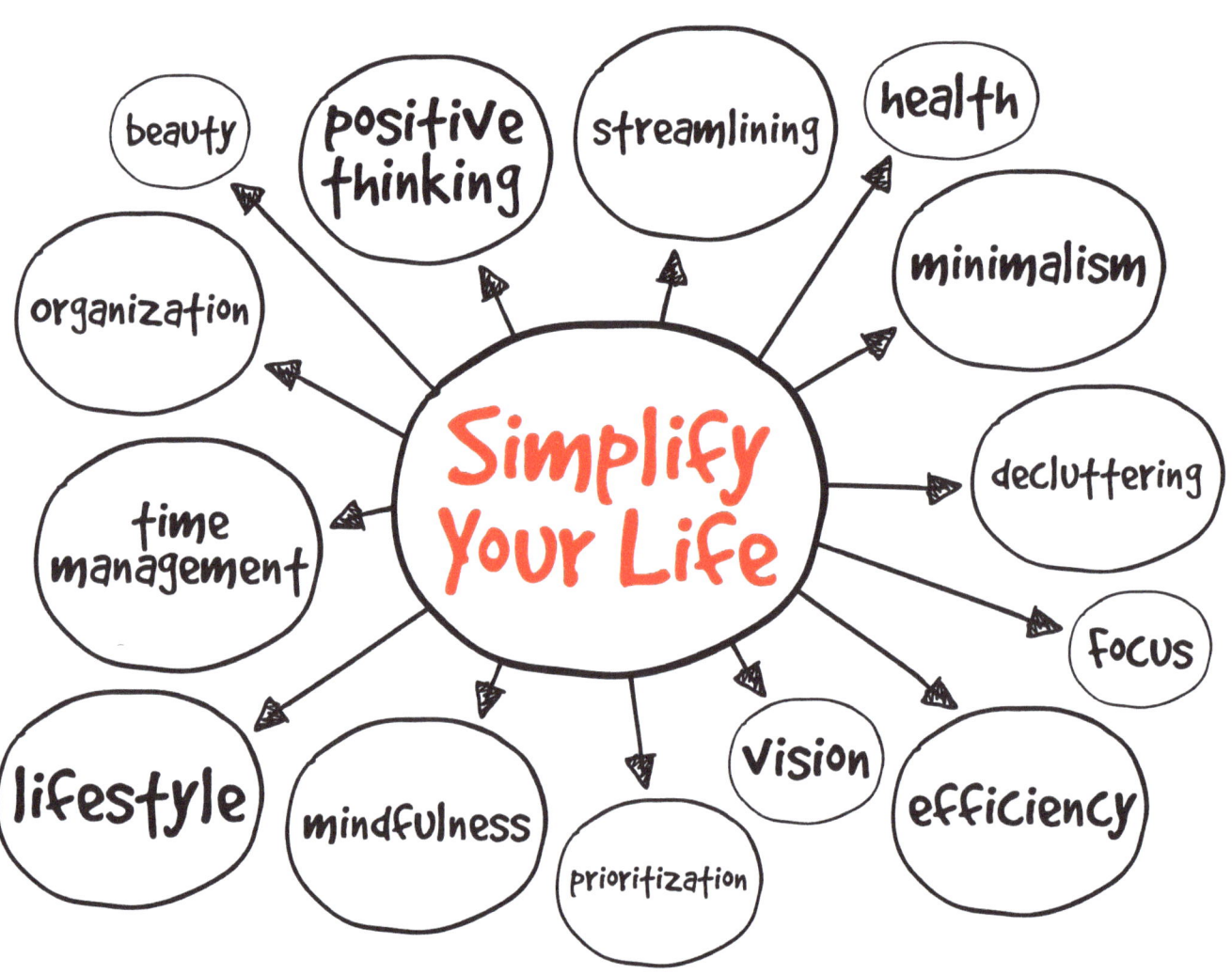

**Organize #OneThing in your home space before walking out the door. A Markism is "a whole lot of little goes a long way!"**

For me, at any time, more order translates into clearer thinking, sharper focus, and less stress. #PlainAndSimple

Whether it's tidying up a desk, making your bed (#RepeatMessagingAsYourFriend), decluttering your fridge, or arranging that one thing that is constantly annoying you, organizing one thing in your home space can give you a momentous sense of order and accomplishment. This easy act can have #PositiveRipples all day long!

This practice aligns with my Markism: "A whole lot of little goes a long way!" It's a reminder that small actions, when done consistently, can lead to game-changers. Organizing one thing each day might not seem like much, but over time, it can significantly improve the cleanliness and Zen of your home. Your pet will appreciate it, also! I know Champ does!

Moreover, an organized space can lead to an organized mind and greatly drive your productivity.

May this inspire you to make a habit of organizing one thing in your home space each day and to appreciate the benefits this small act can deliver to you.

> *"For every minute spent in organizing, an hour is earned."*
> — **Benjamin Franklin**

**Restate your #PositiveAffirmation for the day. #RepeatMessaging is our encouraging dear friend.**

By restating your positive affirmation, you're reinforcing its powerful message to the one living your life, YOU!

For sure, #RepeatMessaging should have priority status in our #SelfTalk. Repetition can enhance memory and influence behavior and actions that are positive and truly meaningful to you. #InputEqualsOutput

Restating your positive affirmation is not just about repetition; it's about demonstrating #SelfCommitment and seeding belief. #MustardSeed

> *"It's the repetition of affirmations that leads to belief. And once that belief becomes a deep conviction, things begin to happen."*
> **—Muhammad Ali**

**Before you walk out the door, visualize yourself coming back victorious, according to your own definition of success, including achieving the #SmallThings that could matter the most.**

Paint that partially blank canvas (because this day is fresh) and create a mental image of your desired outcomes for the day. Seeing is believing. In certain ways, you will imagine success while recognizing potential obstacles that could hinder it.

The key here is to visualize success according to your own definition of it. Success means different things to different people, and it's important to align your visualization with your personal values, aspirations, and reality.

This visualization is catalyzed through action in the first a.m.! Your actions in the morning set the tone for the rest of the day. They can either bring you closer to success or push you further away from it.

Today, for instance, I am visualizing making three important calls to Kansas City contacts when I am in Kansas City by 3 p.m. central time (I am flying there right now on a 6 a.m. flight).

> *"Whatever the mind can conceive and believe, it can achieve."*
> **— Napoleon Hill, author**

**Before you walk out the door, you have nourished the mind, body, and spirit; loved yourself and loved others; identified what you are grateful for and worrying about; and taken atleast one step to be more organized.**

CONGRATULATIONS! You are influencing and advancing your own energy with simple, uncomplicated tips that will #SelfFuelYourExcellence.

It's about self-driven and holistic self-care plus caring for your mind, body, and spirit. You are expressing two of the most precious emotions: love and gratitude . . . and all by 9 a.m.!

These simple routines are not just about doing things but about nurturing the #BestOfYou. The results are all wins: more love, more gratitude, more discipline, more grit, more vulnerability to fuel more strength, more self-care, more order, and, hopefully, more hope and happiness. And, of course, MORE ENERGY!

> *"The secret of your future is hidden in your daily routine."*
> **—Mike Murdock, singer, songwriter and televangelist**

**"LIVE A GREAT STORY®," not only in good times but also in bad times. In all its beauty and complexity, life is a precious gift; accordingly, you are gifted.**

"LIVE A GREAT STORY©" is one of my top five phrases. "LIVE A GREAT STORY©" in good times and bad times. This is a powerful reminder that life, in all its ups and downs, is a journey to be embraced. Every moment, every experience, every challenge, and every triumph are a part of your unique story.

Living a great story doesn't mean striving for perfection or avoiding hardship. It means embracing life in all its complexity, learning from every experience, and growing stronger with each challenge. It's about finding beauty in the ordinary, courage in the face of adversity, and joy overall with the precious gift of life.

In all its beauty and complexity, life is a precious gift. And accordingly, you are gifted. Don't just be a passive observer of your life; be the author of your own story.

*"LIVE A GREAT STORY©"*
—Zach Horvath, founder and owner

**Claim #YourSelfFueledEnergy and #WinTheDay!**

CONGRATULATIONS!

Through your own simple, uncomplicated, and self-directed actions, you are on your way to "this little light of mine; I'm gonna let it shine." You have created and fueled your own energy by 9 a.m.!

Remember, winning the day doesn't necessarily mean achieving everything on your to-do list, reaching a major milestone, or implementing all twenty-one tips. It means applying these simple principles, habituating them, and improving the chances of your success AS YOU—not others—DEFINE IT. It means living your great story, not just in good times but also in bad times.

So, claim your energy, embrace the day, and remember, you are gifted. Trust me, life will be more fulfilling, purposeful, and meaningful.

These straightforward, uncomplicated, and ready-to-implement tips are all acts of self-empowerment that, when turned into habits, have the power to transform your life. They are like mustard seeds of potential that you sow within yourself, for yourself. Remember, dreams can and do come true. I stand as a testament to this truth. Each day, each moment, you have the opportunity to shape your life with these seeds of hope. Embrace them, and watch as your life blossoms into the dream you've always envisioned.

Thank you for taking this journey together.

As for a closing quote, consider this:

> *"The biggest adventure you can ever take is to live the life of your dreams."* **—Oprah Winfrey**

# CONCLUSION

It's important to remember that everyone, regardless of their current circumstances or feelings, has the capacity to make positive changes in their lives. These uncomplicated tips are not just for those already feeling their best but also for those struggling or feeling vulnerable.

For those who are feeling down or going through a tough time, remember that it's okay to start small. Maybe you're not ready to embrace all these practices at once, and that's perfectly fine. At the very least, choose one that resonates with you and start there. The beauty of my principles is that they can be applied by anyone, regardless of their circumstances. Everyone has the potential to harness their energy, exercise discipline, and demonstrate grit to live their best life.

Perhaps you begin by identifying one thing you're grateful for each day. This can help shift your focus from what's going wrong to what's going right. Or maybe you start by making your bed each morning, giving you a small sense of accomplishment to start your day.

Remember, "A whole lot of little goes a long way!" Each small step you take is a victory, a sign of your strength and resilience. And with each step, you're moving closer to a brighter, more positive future.

Everyone has the capacity for greatness, and that includes you. No

matter how you feel right now, know that you deserve happiness and success. These uncomplicated tips are tools to help you realize that.

So, remember: "A whole lot of little goes a long way!" Each small step you take is a victory, a sign of your strength and resilience. And with each step, you're moving closer to a brighter, more positive future. So, claim your energy, embrace the journey, and go forth and win the day! You've got this.

For those days when it feels too hard, remember this quote:

> *"You are braver than you believe, stronger than you seem, and smarter than you think."* **—A.A. Milne**

# REFERENCES

- Cleveland Clinic. Circadian Rhythm, March 15, 2024. https://my.clevelandclinic.org/health/articles/circadian-rhythm.

- Crosswalk Editorial Staff. "The Serenity Prayer: Original Version, Author, and Bible Truths." Crosswalk.com, October 6, 2022. https://www.crosswalk.com/faith/prayer/serenity-prayer-applying-3-truths-from-the-bible.html.

- Ruby Lathon, PhD. "6 Things Drinking 2 Glasses of Water Each Morning Does for Your Body!" rubylathon.com, March 30, 2017. https://www.rubylathon.com/single-post/2017/03/30/6-Things-Drinking-2-Glasses-of-Water-each-Morning-Does-for-Your-Body.

# ABOUT THE AUTHOR

**Mark L. Madrid** is an accomplished business strategist, author, and transformative leader, recognized across multiple sectors, including corporate America, Fortune 500, Wall Street, nonprofit, academia, and the federal government. His expertise is sought by companies, organizations, and individuals aiming for breakthroughs, advancement, and results.

Mark's recent venture, Breakthrough Mavens, LLC, provides potent, turnkey, and uncomplicated fractional C-Suite services, infusing his core values of energy, discipline, and grit. These principles form the bedrock of his debut book series, *Self-Fueling Excellence*, with the first edition emphasizing energy.

An alumnus of the University of Texas at Austin and the University of Notre Dame, Mark's commitment to excellence and integrity drives his work, purpose, and philanthropy. He believes in the transformative power of positive energy and the importance of discipline and grit in achieving success. His work is not just about achieving business growth but also about inspiring individuals to reach their full potential.

Mark's unique and accessible approach to leadership, combined with his contagious energy, fanatic discipline, and unwavering grit have empowered countless organizations and individuals to achieve breakthrough success.

www.ingramcontent.com/pod-product-compliance
Lightning Source LLC
Chambersburg PA
CBHW041413010526
44107CB00016B/1152